Our Remarkable Memory

Life is all memory, except for the one
present moment that goes by you so quick
you hardly catch it going.
                                    — Tennessee Williams

OUR REMARKABLE
MEMORY

understanding it • improving it • losing it?

Second Edition

EDITH NALLE SCHAFER

STARRHILL PRESS
Washington & Philadelphia

For my wise and humorous family:
Jack, Beetie, John, Nancy

Published by Starrhill Press
P.O. Box 32342
Washington, DC 20007
(202) 686-6703

For his patience, resourcefulness and erudition, I am grateful to
E. J. Applewhite. To Dr. Trey Sunderland and Dr. Gary Gottlieb,
my thanks for their helpful guidance and for news from the
front.

— E.N.S.

For permission to reprint the Memory Survey on page 69, we
thank the *Washington Post*.

Library of Congress Cataloging-in-Publication Data

    Our remarkable memory: understanding it, improving it,
losing it?
  / Edith Nalle Schafer. — 2nd ed.
      p.   cm.
    Includes bibliographical references and index.
    ISBN 0-913515-82-5
    1. Memory. 2. Memory disorders. 3. Mnemonics.   Title.
  QP406.S47   1992
  153.1'2—dc20

                                  92-88

Cover illustration by James McFarlane
Text illustrations by Jonel Sofian

Printed in the United States of America

Second edition

5 4 3 2 1

Contents

continued . . .

Introduction

They are passing, posthaste, posthaste, the
gliding years.... The years are passing, my dear,
and presently no one will know what you and I know.
— Vladimir Nabokov
Speak Memory

Ah, memory. We cherish it, and rightly so. It is the landscape inside our heads, a past where we are at home, a world uniquely and privately our own. It is our country, and when we wander freely and familiarly in it, it assures us that we are the same person in spite of the passage of time. We use the past to define ourselves, to deal with the present, and to prepare for the future. Memory dictates the way we express ourselves, think about ourselves, communicate with others; it is at the core of being human. Just about everything we do depends on our ability to retrieve information from memory. Without memory we could not survive.

Forgetting undermines our confidence and our competence. It threatens our ability to function. Without memory we would have to discover everything anew every day. We would be like the profoundly amnesic H.M., who is described later in this book—able to read the same magazine over and over and find it ever fascinating, always new, seen, as it were, for the first time. We would eat lunch twice, not remembering that we had already eaten it. We would smile pleasantly and recognize no one that we hadn't seen in the last few minutes. We would be prisoners of the present, while the rich accumulations of our lives, our varied and interesting selves, would be missing.

Men have eaten walnuts, fish, and tribal chieftains in hope of acquiring memory benefits or superior mental abilities. Probably none of these efforts was effective. Human memory is vastly more complex and fascinating than we have suspected. Memory is elegant and powerful; it is also fallible.

In our understanding of the human brain, we are Renaissance mariners with a sixteenth-century map in a vast and numinous ocean. We perceive fairly well the outline of the dark continent of memory, but its interior is murky, not well marked and only fitfully illuminated. The cartographers configure it differently every year. Some three pounds of grayish-pink jelly—our dazzling, inscrutable brain with all its stylish accomplishments—may be the most complicated piece of equipment in the universe. But all we have to study the human brain with is the human brain. Can the brain know itself?

Slowly, perhaps it can. Concern for the memory-related problems of an aging population has led to increased study of this function of the brain. When memory is better understood, research will concentrate on language—the sending and receiving of messages—and we should take another step forward in understanding ourselves.

Understanding ourselves. The following pages will look at what we know, and also at what we surmise, about brain function and the workings of memory. They will touch on how we historically have tried to understand the phenomenon of memory and how we are still trying. Different sections will consider memory and the law; collective memory or the memory of the human race; the uses of forgetting; and forms of memory loss, in particular, Alzheimer's disease. The final section will offer coping tips, strategies for remembering, and mnemonic devices.

The news is better than you think, and worse.

I THINK, THEREFORE I REMEMBER
Cognition

Perception is a basic component of memory. What do you see here—an attractive young woman or a gnarled old woman?

How much do we know about how memory works? To begin with there is cognition, which involves many mental processes including paying attention, perceiving, learning, making decisions, thinking, problem solving, and memory. Memory is the most fundamental building block of cognition. Nothing that we do that involves cognition takes place in the absence of memory. When we pay attention we use memory to tell us what to attend to. When we perceive we're drawing on information represented in memory as a basis for understanding what it is we see out there, and so on through all the other elements of cognition. Scientists have not yet been able to break cognition down into its component parts, but there are lots of clues.[1]

The science of cognition studies the brain as processor of information. It seeks to understand human intelligence and how people think. While we may not be able to improve our intelligence or our memories, we *are* able to use the equipment we have more effectively. What we are now learning about cognition will have large implications for our intellectual performance by the turn of the century. We will surely and sorely need increased capacity and efficiency as the information explosion and the technological revolution put ever greater demands on our cognitive processes.

> We are an intelligent species and the use of our intelligence quite properly gives us pleasure. In this respect the brain is like a muscle. When it is in use we feel very good. Understanding is joyous.
> — Carl Sagan
> *Broca's Brain*

THE THREE-LAYERED BRAIN

The human brain weighs about three pounds. Ironed out, it would be roughly the size of a sheet of newsprint. To fit into the skull it has to be highly convoluted. Human brains are much more folded and coiled than those of other animals.[2]

The critical mass of the human brain, and also the most recently evolved portion, is the cerebral cortex or neocortex. It contains three quarters of the neurons in the brain and is the seat of thinking, judgment, speech, and memory. It is what makes us human.

The neocortex is the third and latest brain layer in the three-layer-brain theory set forth by Dr. Paul MacLean of the National Institute of Mental Health. These three interconnected brain layers reflect our ancestral relationships to reptiles, to early mammals, and to later mammals.[3]

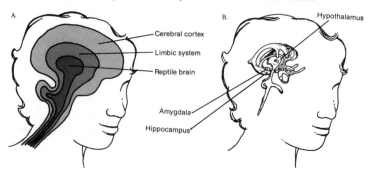

A. Configuration of the three-layered brain.

B. The limbic system —the amygdala and the hippocampus— which is heavily involved in the process of memory. Closely connected to the hypothalamus, these structures deal with emotions.

The "second brain" is the limbic system, which deals with emotions. The limbic system includes the amygdala and the hippocampus, a small, seahorse-shaped organ that forms long-term memories. Both depend on an intricate network of sensory connections, and both are closely connected to the olfactory system. All of our sensations can evoke memory, none more strongly than taste and smell.

The hippocampus, which is central to the operation of memory, seems to integrate separate perceptions as they occur into a single memorable experience.[4] The amygdala doesn't process memory but rather deals with emotions, and emotions play a major role in what we remember. Though there is ample evidence that memory is stored all over the brain, damage to the limbic system has a devastating effect on storing and retrieving events and emotions.

The oldest or "reptile brain" is an expansion of the upper brain stem. It is responsible for such responses as hunting, mating, fighting, self-defense, sociability, and following leaders.

> My mother, seeing that I was cold, offered me some tea. And soon, mechanically, weary after a dull day with the prospect of a depressing morrow, I raised to my lips a spoonful of the tea in which I had soaked a morsel of the cake. No sooner had the warm liquid, and the crumbs with it, touched my palate than a shudder ran through my whole body. . . . An exquisite pleasure had invaded my senses. . . . Suddenly the memory returns . . . the whole of Combray and its surroundings, taking their proper shapes and growing solid, sprang into being, town and gardens alike, from my cup of tea.
> — Marcel Proust
> *Remembrance of Things Past*

WATCHING MEMORY WORK

From time to time advances in understanding are made that are in the nature of revelations.

At a conference of neuroscientists in New Orleans in the fall of 1991 a breakthrough as surprising as it was exciting was announced. A sophisticated X-ray scanner had been able to photograph the human brain as it performed various memory tasks (in this case, recalling words). A research team led by Dr. Marcus Raichle of Washington University was able to watch recollection happening and to sort out that activity from all the other activities of a brain at work.

Using positron emission tomography (PET scan), scientists followed the course of blood that had been injected with a slightly radioactive dye so that it glowed faintly as it traveled through the body, including to and around the brain. When cells become active they burn up more sugar than usual, and this process creates more blood flow in the regions at work. Concentrations of marked blood showed up as "hot spots," which the scientists identified as the parts of the brain that were most active during various tasks. They saw parts of the brain actually *light up* with memory, and the activity switched from place to place as the different parts communicated with each other or worked simultaneously, "humming and fading in many spots like fireflies in a tree."[5]

"Given the subtlety of cognition, it's a surprise you can see anything at all," said Dr. Larry Squire, an author of the paper that reported these findings. "It augurs well for using PET to get at the secrets of the brain."[6]

Some tasks involved only perception—recognizing shapes. These lit up the visual area in the back of the head.

Some engaged conscious memory. These lit up the prefrontal cortex, which seemed to be directing the memory search carried out by the middle brain.

"Priming," one of dozens of distinct brain functions, occurs when a subject has seen a picture or heard a word recently but has no conscious recollection of it. When there has been priming, less work, less neural activity, needs to take place to recall the word or picture. (Oddly enough, people with severe amnesia perform memory tasks well after priming. When the brain knows something cold, it apparently doesn't have to work very hard to recall it. In fact, the less thinking the brain did, the better memory worked.[7])

Another revelation from the PET scan is that memory involves several areas of the brain at once; many little information processors are linked together in a complex network. Memory is numerous separate abilities carried out in separate places in the brain.

Over the centuries memory has been studied in abnormal brains or damaged brains by seeking to isolate the damaged areas in order to understand the deficit and, almost by subtraction, what was left and where and why certain things took place. Now research can be done on healthy brains performing normal remembering.

"The information from this technique is unbeatable," says Dr. Mortimer Mishkin of the National Institute of Mental Health. "It has just opened a window on the brain that we did not dream of 10 or 15 years ago."[8]

THE MAGIC LOOM

How the brain actually functions is to some extent still a mystery, but the process seems to go something like this: the basic unit of transmission is the neuron, the most important cell in the brain for information processing. An electro-chemical impulse is received by a dendrite and travels to the end of the neuron to the axon (think of it as a wire), where it triggers the release of a neurotransmitter. This liquid chemical messenger flows across the gap or synapse (from the Greek verb, "to clasp") to a receptor, passing along the news, which in turn triggers the next neuron to fire an impulse of its own, and so on and on and on. The complexity of the human brain lies in the vast number of synapses (connections) between brain cells. The profusion of interconnections among the cells is beyond

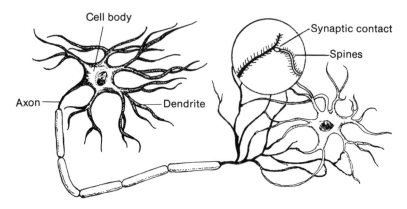

Synaptic contact between two neurons in the brain—two of the some ten billion we each have.

human imagining. (Again, can the brain fully define itself?) Picture some ten billion neurons each receiving connections from perhaps a hundred others, each of which is connected with a hundred others. The transmission of a "wave front" may sweep over a hundred thousand neurons in a second, operating on both nearby cells and those in distant parts of the cortex.[9]

To put this in some kind of perspective, there are more neurons in the brain than there are stars in the Milky Way. There are maybe a trillion, and each of them can talk to maybe a thousand other cells making 10^{15} connections. (A trillion is a figure so large that it would take 32,000 years to count to it saying one number per second.) Or to put it another way, the brain has the information-processing power of a hundred billion medium-size interacting computers.[10] Dr. Charles Scott Sherrington, the English neurophysiologist who introduced the term "synapse," called the brain an "enchanted loom where millions of flashing shuttles weave a dissolving pattern, always a meaningful pattern though never an abiding one, a shifting harmony of subpatterns."

The mysteries of the mind are only beginning to give way to our understanding of the physico-chemical properties of the brain. Can we ultimately make the connection between personality and chemistry? Every human yearning is a result of chemical interaction between transmitters and receptors, says Jon Franklin in *Molecules of the Mind*.[11] So much for all our fancy thinking, our courage, our subtle and powerful emotions, our piety and wit.

> One has been endowed with just enough
> intelligence to be able to see clearly how
> inadequate that intelligence is when confronted
> with what exists.
> — Albert Einstein

WILL WE EVER GET IT RIGHT?
Understanding Ourselves

Memory was held in such high esteem by the ancient Greeks that they made Mnemosyne, the Goddess of Memory, the mother of all the muses. It was she who ruled over Calliope (Epic Poetry), Clio (History), Euterpe (Flute Playing), Melpomene (Tragedy), Terpsichore (Dancing), Erato (the Lyre), Polyhymnia (Sacred Song), Urania (Astronomy), and Thalia (Comedy). Memory reigned over all: everyone needed memory, everyone had to cultivate and perfect his own.

The Greek poet Simonides of Ceos was said to be the inventor of the mnemonic art. At a banquet in Thessaly, Simonides happened to be outside when the roof of the hall collapsed, killing everyone inside. When the grieving relatives came to claim the shattered bodies, Simonides, because of his excellent memory, was able to recall where each guest had been sitting and thus to identify the bodies.

The Greeks and Romans often used imaginary placement in a house as a mnemonic device. Placement and image were the blocks with which they built their memory skills. The first thing they wished to remember was mentally placed in the entrance hall, and so on through the whole house. So it is that today, when we have organized our thoughts, we often say, "In the first place . . . "

Before the advent of writing, the memory of individuals carried knowledge down through the years and across seas and continents. The epic poems of antiquity, the *Iliad* and the *Odyssey,* were part of an oral tradition. English common law was preserved in the memory of the community; it was a collection of customs that were accepted because "the memory of man runneth not to the contrary." To this day, cultures without a written history rely on the memory of a *griot* or village elder who is a designated repository of the community's past.

The rise of the art of writing, and later of printing, rapidly devalued the art of memory. When citizens could refer to books to ascertain the law or the rules of grammar or the liturgy, prodigious feats of memory became mere stunts.[12] Einstein couldn't remember his own phone number. Was this a problem for him? Not at all. He could, he said, always look up the number when he needed it.

Early Gropings

From earliest times we have been trying to locate memory and then to understand how this tricky, useful faculty actually works. Some suggested that memory was in the liver, others that it was in the spine or the retina. Aristotle thought the heart was the thinking organ and the brain's function was to cool the blood. Reason and emotion, argued the Greeks, were to be found in the "gut," somewhere in the midsection, and no one knew what to make of "that puzzling thing in the head."[13] From Plato until the early 1900s, memory was thought of as an impression in wax—"the mark of the thing"—just as the imprint of a fern frond laid in soft mud persists, or as a once folded piece of paper is easier to fold again.

Through the Middle Ages Simonides' idea of remembering things by placement and image held sway. In fact, it is still in use today. Few troubled themselves with how the confusing process actually worked. Then in the sixteenth century, just about the time Copernicus established the sun as the center of our planetary system, Vesalius, a surgeon and anatomist revolutionary enough to cut up dead bodies to see how they were put together, took mental processes away from the heart and gave them to the brain. Where they remain to this day.

The march of science was temporarily sidetracked when Franz Joseph Gall (1758-1828), a German physician, advanced his belief that the shape of the head was the key to what was going on inside. Bumps and protuberances were centers of knowledge or character traits; protruding eyeballs indicated a good memory. So began phrenology. While this pseudoscience was destined for disgrace, it prefigured the idea that certain areas of the brain controlled certain functions.

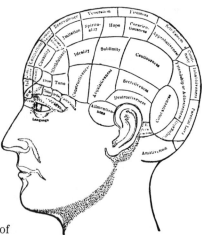

Phrenologist's diagram of the brain giving a specific location for each of the following:

Human Nature	Tune	Combativeness
Agreeableness	Mirthfulness	Destructiveness
Comparison	Causality	Secretiveness
Eventuality	Benevolence	Cautiousness
Locality	Veneration	Approbativeness
Individuality	Firmness	Acquisitiveness
Size	Self-Esteem	Constructiveness
Form	Continuity	Sublimity
Weight	Inhibitiveness	Ideality
Language	Parental Love	Imitation
Color	Amativeness	Spirituality
Order	Conjugality	Hope
Calculation	Friendship or	Consciousness
Time	Adhesiveness	Alimentiveness

Herman Ebbinghaus, a German psychologist, undertook studies in the measurement of memory and in 1885 wrote a classic monograph called *Memory, A Contribution to Experimental Psychology.* In his experiments he used nonsense syllables (*zof, vum, hiu, leq,* etc.) in order to eliminate meaningfulness of material, personal biases, and motivations. Ebbinghaus was criticized for unscientific testing (he used only one subject—himself), but his work was a watershed in the understanding of memory.

This is the use of memory: for liberation . . . liberation from the future as well as the past.
— T. S. Eliot

Ebbinghaus was able to plot a memory curve indicating that the memory proceeds rapidly in the beginning and tapers off gradually. The curve showed that some memory is retained indefinitely. Long pieces of poetry memorized as a young man, and then dismissed from mind, were quickly relearned some twenty years later, demonstrating that material learned once is relatively easily learned again.

The next giant in the study of memory was Sir Frederick Bartlett, author of *Remembering* (1932), whose studies emphasized the importance of meaning to memory. His research encouraged his subjects to build on their own experiences, associations, and attitudes and thus take advantage of patterns of meaning they had already developed. The idea of putting information in an orderly structure proved to be a useful one, and Bartlett's use of the term "schema" for a body of knowledge on a specific topic has computer applications today.

Experimental physiologist Karl Lashley (1890-1958) spent twenty years looking for the place in the brain where memory is stored. To this end he trained rats to navigate a maze, then removed selective parts of their brains. Even though the brain operations produced various deficits, the animals always remembered how to find their way through the maze. He had not been able to remove their memory; it had proved elusive again.[14]

The twentieth century has approached the study of memory through its pathology. How and why does memory fail?[15] The subject of forgetting has become the frontier of modern psychology. Latent memory, otherwise known as the unconscious, has not lacked for attention in our time. And what about dreams, that vast storehouse of memories in disguise? Said Dr. Freud, "In mental life nothing which has once been formed can perish. . . . Everything is somehow preserved." It is all in there. If it is bothering us, somehow it needs to be gotten out. Freud's "talking cure" is essentially remembering. The art of memory becomes the key to self-discovery.[16] Psychoanalysis and Mnemosyne dance hand in hand.

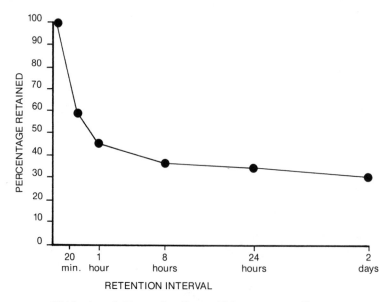

Ebbinghaus's Forgetting Curve. This pattern applies to many types of learned material.

BRAIN MODELS

Human beings like to make analogies between the brain and their latest invention or interest. In earlier, and possibly more bellicose, times the military analogy was popular. Thus the forebrain and the limbic system made plans and issued commands that ultimately were followed by the spinal cord, whose task was simply to obey. In the seventeenth century, the mind was seen as a lens or a mirror, focusing and reflecting thoughts. It was thought of as a tabula rasa, a blank piece of paper upon which experience writes. After the Industrial Revolution the mind became a machine, or even a whole factory. With the invention of the telephone it became a switchboard, sending and receiving messages. In post-World War II America we have a bureaucratic turn of mind, seeing hierarchies, chains of command, and flow charts. Most recently the computer is our model, and we talk of input and output, programming and feedback.

Our next brain model appears to be the hologram, which involves photography and lasers and expresses the concept that any fragment can reproduce the whole, that the retrieval of any part of an experience will call forth the entire experience. Because the information on a holographic plate is distributed, a somewhat degraded reconstruction of the whole stored image can be retrieved, even if part of the plate is lost. Memories are stored all over the brain, and the most minute particle of any single memory contains a code for accessing the whole.[17]

In fact, no analogy is particularly useful because the brain is unique. There is nothing else like it.

THE WAY IT WORKS

Encoding

Memory is the process of storing and retrieving information. We learn by committing information to memory. Scientists speak of short-term memory (STM) and long-term memory (LTM); there is a point at which long-term memory becomes learning. Human memory has three components: encoding, storage, and retrieval. Encoding is getting the information in there; it involves extracting information from experience; it is the representation of one thing by another. Storage is the persistence of encoded information over time. Retrieval is utilization of stored material.

So, input, storage, and output are the operations of memory, as of the computer. The first step in getting something into memory is paying attention, attending to it. This step is absolutely essential. Before we can remember we must perceive; we can't forget what we never got in the first place. Encoding can involve setting information in a matrix of associations, thus reinforcing it. Classifying it, arranging it in some kind of order, visualizing it, repeating it, and rehearsing it can be helpful. We do two things: (1) individual event processing and (2) relational processing, relating separate events to one another. We do these steps automatically when the subject is of interest and concern to us, more consciously when we set about learning something.

Information first enters our consciousness through sensory memory. This form of memory takes in everything we perceive and is of very short duration—maybe a second. That we hold it even ever so briefly justifies calling it a memory; it's a message that stays on the edge of consciousness. Sensory memory includes iconic memory (for visual information) and echoic memory (for auditory information). A great deal of the information that gets into sensory memory is rapidly lost if it is not attended to. Thus paying attention is key to retaining information long enough for further processing.

You think you are observant? Which one is it?

Attention is a very limited mental resource. We have trouble attending to two demanding things at the same time. Consider how difficult it is to carry on two conversations at once (the cocktail party syndrome) or simultaneously to add two columns of figures. So, only that portion of sensory memory that is attended to is ready for the next stage—short-term memory.

Short-term memory is the capacity for keeping a limited amount of information in a special active state; this information is accessible only when it is in this active state. STM has severe time constraints on it. We are talking about fifteen seconds, and even then you have to rehearse the information in order not to lose it, as one repeats a telephone number until it can be dialed. Telephone numbers have seven digits or components; seven is the average number of information bits we can retain in STM. Sometimes it's nine and sometimes only five; we can retain more if we can chunk bits of information together. Chunking can be done in various ways: by pausing as we do between the third and fourth digits in phone numbers, by rhyme, by rhythm, or by sensible and reasonable groupings. Nonsense syllables, meaningless and unrelated, are hardest to retain.

Rehearsal, or repetition, or just keeping something in mind, prepares information for more permanent storage. The transition from STM to LTM—encoding—entails turning information into electrical impulses by a process that is not yet fully understood. The electrical impulse flashing across the dense web of neurons makes a pattern that is called an engram or, more commonly, a memory trace. Encoding is the word contemporary psychologists use to describe how we extract information from experience. The final product that gets stored is in a highly abstracted form and many synapses removed from the original stimulus.[18] Perhaps memories are converted to peptides, and strings of amino acid units carry a loved grandparent's familiar features in coded form. We don't really know yet just how it works.[19]

If there is a central concept in encoding it is contextualism. This is the idea that what we store depends on the context in which we experience events, and this means not only the external context—the physical reality we find ourselves in—but the internal context as well. In other words, the emotional climate we bring with us predisposes us to find some events more significant than others. Says Canadian psychologist Endel Tulving, "Our cognitive environment, what we know, what we have in our head at the time we experience any event will determine the kind of information we extract from events and the kind of information we store in memory."

To remember better, reinstate the context at the time of encoding. Without carrying this idea too far, let's just say that lists of words learned under water are better remembered under water. Events that occurred while drinking which cannot be recalled sober may come back when drunk again. This is called state-dependent learning. Reinstate the context at the time of retention—a bleak study hall, a flowery meadow, an automobile accident—and more is remembered. It can also be useful to reinstate the mood one was in

We think the flow of information in memory goes something like this:

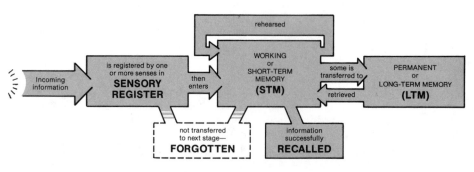

at the time of encoding. (More on this in Eyewitness Reporting.)

Depth of encoding is directly related to depth of processing. Processing *time* isn't the major factor in getting information into memory, *depth* of processing is. Paying attention, being touched or enraged, repeating—that's depth of processing. That's what makes things stick.

Once information has been sufficiently processed, successfully processed, so that it is really in there, it can survive coma, electroconvulsive shock, extreme cold, even some forms of brain damage, as we shall see. It seems that this kind of successful encoding results in changes in the structure of the brain itself; LTM can produce lasting structural changes in the pathways of the cells. Therefore we must think of the brain as plastic, not static, with some synapses that are mature, some developing, some regressing. Learning something may stimulate growth of dendritic spines and synapses, improving their performance; disuse of the mind encourages their erosion and loss.

A Greek definition of happiness: the exercise of vital powers along lines of excellence in a life affording them scope.

Storage

Long-term memory and short-term memory are both working on getting information into storage: "LTM is responsible for making permanent records that are available to consciousness at short notice; for making sense of the records in the light of what's already stored there; and for their constant updating in the light of new information. In addition, it helps STM with the third remembering step: finding the required material."[20] When you need it.

How does the brain select out what to remember? Emotional factors play a large part. Emotions are closely involved with the limbic system. Strong feelings and stress act as fixatives, triggering the release of adrenalin and other brain chemicals. Intense or profound experiences get attention. Thus things that are biologically or emotionally important tend to be remembered.

Memory has a bias in favor of affirmative answers: we remember better if the answer is yes; we do less of the necessary processing when the answer is no. Fullness of life enhances memory. Studies done on rich versus impoverished cognitive environments demonstrate that rats with fuller lives have more nerve cells in the brain, a heavier brain and better memory capacities than deprived rats. We, too, benefit from stimulating environments. They provide cognitive benefits for old people just as they do for the very young. Curiosity, activity, involvement create rich schemas.

Schemas are tightly structured bodies of knowledge. They are all the circumstances we know concerning a given activity. For instance, we have a schema for going to a restaurant: certain things are quite likely to happen, and in a certain order. We also have a schema for washing the car or going to the beach—reasonable expectations of what will happen. This knowledge of what tends to occur in certain circumstances is important to our ability to predict what we will encounter in our environment. Our schemas allow us to interpret our experience and to represent the information in memory in several ways.

Computers can have a schema or a script for going to a restaurant, too—a set of expectations—but the world is richer than any script you can give a computer, because the world can't be described fully. It has to be perceived. No matter how large the computer's script is, you know more, because you've lived in the world.

Besides, computers lack judgment and haven't much sense of humor.

Chess illustrates nicely the relationship between human and artificial memory. A good human player sees patterns at a glance, a computer checks all the possibilities—fast. It's a good player, but it doesn't get any better, it doesn't learn. The brain is incomprehensibly more complex than a computer. Therefore the bottom line on artificial intelligence is that a human being is a human being, and a computer is a piece of hardware.[21]

Back to the Grand Masters. They don't even need a board; they can carry it all in their heads. Take it a step further and consider this: with ESP they wouldn't even need language in order to play; a game of chess would consist of one brain sending messages to another brain.

The pros have a richly articulated schema, or matrix, with access to memory clues. However, if chessmen are placed at random on a board, the pros are no better at recreating the board once it is removed than the novice because the placement of the men no longer makes sense.

The point is it's easier to learn about something you are interested in or to learn more about a subject you already know something about. Run a tape of a baseball game and then give the audience a test on what they have seen. The baseball fans will remember the events they have seen better than the others and the fans will be able to infer things that might not have appeared on the tape. Their internal cognitive environment is an important aid to remembering. Common sense and intuition would indicate this, of course, but it is also clearly born out by studies. Chance favors the prepared mind.

Honeybees, with brains that weigh 1/1000 of a gram, have STM and LTM for the location of a certain kind of flower at a certain time of day. Later in the day they may have memory for a new location and a different kind of flower, but never both at once. They are specialists. They have to be, that's all they have room for.

—Jeremy Campbell
Winston Churchill's
Afternoon Nap

Retrieval

The third component of memory, retrieval, is getting information out of storage. It involves the conscious processes of recognition and recall—the output of memory. Recognition occurs when there is a realization that a present situation is parallel to a former one. A recognition question is easier than a recall question because it offers more network paths (associations) to be searched for the information. Multiple choice questions, which offer clues, are generally easier than essay questions.

Recall brings things back by connections. For example, compare the following questions:

Who was president before Lincoln?

Was Buchanan president before Lincoln?

In the first instance the request is to recall, first accessing Lincoln and then searching for Buchanan. If the network between Lincoln and Buchanan is weak, too weak to be activated, recall fails. The second question, which requests recognition, is considerably easier. When people complain about forgetting, they mean failure to recall, not failure to recognize.[22]

The amygdala and hippocampus's real job is associative memory. When we can link a memory to more than one memory trace, our chances of getting it out of storage increase dramatically. Linkage, or association, plays a big part in recall. Think of it as a cross-referencing system. When we can't remember a man's name immediately, we think about where he lives or how we met him, activating networks of associations until we arrive at his name. These semantic networks, or networks of associated meanings, facilitate recall. Conversely, isolated facts are more easily forgotten.

In conversation, with its simultaneous demands on input, storage, and output, it is no wonder that sometimes we make slips of the tongue or lose our train of thought. There is simply a lot going on.

    According to Donald Norman of the University of California, San Diego, "Errors and confusions caused by overload are simply by-products of the powerful and flexible operations of the human mind that also lead to curiosity, discovery and insight."[23]

It was in St. Louis just before the concert was to start that the second bassoonist came to Toscanini in a state of great agitation. He had just discovered that the lowest note on his instrument was broken and there was no time to get it repaired. What was to be done? Toscanini, shading his eyes, thought for a minute and then said, "It's all right—that note does not occur in tonight's concert."

VARIETIES OF MEMORY

Procedural/Declarative

It is necessary to distinguish between two major memory systems: declarative knowledge and procedural knowledge. Declarative knowledge is knowledge about the world and how it works, knowledge about facts and things. Like a computer, you can declare the contents of declarative knowledge and use it to remember specific facts; it provides explicit access to facts. We can dredge up its information when we need it, and its contents can be gotten at in any number of ways.

Procedural knowledge deals with how to perform various activities; it is for the development and expression of skills: riding a bicycle, solving a puzzle, carving a chicken. It includes the rules and operations for solving problems, the how-to part of living. Think of the brain as different sets of processors—visual, auditory, logical, etc. When needed, you tune up these processors and they work in such a way that you don't have to remember how you learned an activity in order to perform it. For instance, when you serve a tennis ball you don't have to remember how or where you learned what to do; you only have to remember how to do it. Our skills are not tied to explicit knowledge of exactly what we do. Typists don't "know"; that is, they don't think about where the keys are, they just type.

Episodic/Semantic

Canadian psychologist Endel Tulving made a further distinction between two types of LTM: episodic memory and semantic memory. Episodic memory stores specific events: a picnic in the woods, or knowledge that the oven is on. It is personal and autobiographical. It is also context- and sequence-related, it includes things that happened ten minutes ago. When and where events took place is important.

Semantic memory includes knowledge of the world: the capital of China, the bidding sequence in bridge, $e = mc^2$, the meaning of words, and so on. It enables us to make sense of the world, to interpret events, to form some organized trace of ongoing events—geography, art, music, objects, language. Semantic memory is independent of the sequence and context in which information occurs.

Whoever in discussion adduces authority uses not intellect but rather memory.

— Leonardo da Vinci

Episodic and semantic memory interact with each other, one putting an emphasis on time, the other not. Semantic memory can be asked, "What is a plane ticket?" Episodic memory can be asked, "Where did you use this plane ticket?"

These terms, episodic/semantic, procedural/declarative, are concepts currently in use in the attempt to break down and understand the workings of memory. The episodic/semantic distinction falls under the declarative memory umbrella; this is the area where most of the research has focused. Concentration on procedural memory, memory for skills, awaits its turn.

Everyday memory performance can't be broken down neatly into these two systems or explained on the basis of the distinction between them. They are different forms of memory, but are they separate systems or different aspects of a single system? There is evidence that they are separate systems because they can be disrupted differently in different diseases, they are altered differently by different drugs, and we gain access to them differently. Episodic memory is deliberate; semantic memory is automatic. Although we cannot dissect memory and spread it out neatly in sections on the laboratory table, it seems that it is not a single process, but many processes. The distinctions between the two systems become important when we begin to examine memory loss.[24]

THE MEMORY OF THE GENES

Just as the individual has a memory, so does the human race. Behavioral scientist Konrad Lorenz says that knowledge enters the organism in two ways: either by evolutionary means through the species, or developmentally through the individual. Evolution is the memory of the genes. "Genes affect the way the mind is formed—which stimuli are perceived and which are missed, how information is processed, the kind of memories most easily recalled, the emotions they are most likely to evoke, and so on."[25]

Each person's memories are absolutely custom-made and private. No one else has them. They are tailored to the individual, products of one's mental disposition and uniqueness of experience. But human beings seem to have known some things all along. We seem to have been programmed with them from the beginning. These things make up Carl Jung's "collective unconscious." Jung believed that our unconscious holds all the deep emotional experiences of mankind since the beginning. Therefore some of the things we do come from our distant biological past; they are survivals of attributes that were useful when they first appeared in evolutionary development.[26]

For instance, the fight-or-flight response, the body's ability to anticipate danger and mobilize its resources, is an attribute not always useful for civilized man. The changes in metabolism and circulation that occur may not be as appropriate for a difference of opinion at the office as they were for fending off genuine predators in the forest.

In the process of natural selection, only the most useful genetic memories are retained. Things that are biologically or emotionally important will be remembered. This emergence of the capacity to learn is the triumph of evolution. We are able to anticipate changes in our environment in the light of what has already happened. Each of us adds our supply of personal secrets to what we know of the world's probabilities. [27]

Human beings have mental memory (what is in their heads) plus the genetic code (what is in their DNA—the genetic material concentrated in the nerve cell nucleus). Scientific experiments using genetic material and the phenomenon of memory suggest that it is possible to inherit knowledge, that it is stored within the nerve cells. The brain therefore deals with a store of inherited knowledge as well as knowledge from individual experience. Our brains can do this fast, efficiently, and with great sophistication.

Memory believes before knowing remembers.
Believes longer than recollects, longer than
knowing even wonders.
— William Faulkner
As I Lay Dying

SOME CURIOUS
MEMORY PHENOMENA

Since Ebbinghaus and Bartlett, memory studies have turned up some interesting phenomena:

• The Reminiscence Effect demonstrates that a student learning twenty-five lines of a long poem today will remember three additional lines tomorrow, even though he has only read through the additional lines and not attempted to memorize them.[28]

• The Zegarnik Effect suggests that better learning takes place if a task is not completed: the brain seems to retain best that which is not yet brought to a conclusion.[28]

• It was a nineteenth-century Scot, Sir William Hamilton, who discovered that the mind could only count six or seven objects instantaneously. Joseph Jacobs, working two years after Ebbinghaus published his book on memory, found that he could memorize only seven or eight digits or objects at one reading. However, fortunately, items can be lumped together (chunking) so that more than seven digits can be retained. Take 149218627231416. Difficult, but not so difficult when it becomes the year we associate with Columbus, the speed of light in miles per second, and the value of pi.[28]

• Canadian neurosurgeon Wilder Penfield, working on a treatment for epilepsy, stimulated the hippocampus and the temporal lobe of the brain of conscious patients with a weak electrical current. Immediately the patients were transported into the past. Episodes and events and people long forgotten appeared vividly before them, including lights and voices—distant and intimate memories from their stream of consciousness—as if they were eavesdropping on a familiar scene.[29]

• Try this experiment. Write the names of five colors in fat letters on separate cards and fill in the letters with some other color. The word red is colored blue, etc. Flash these cards and attempt to say the color, not the word. How did you do? This exercise demonstrates automatic lexical access, called the Stroup Effect. The more familiar the material, the less attention it requires until it requires virtually no attention at all. In many situations we become so practiced that appropriate words will come into our heads unbidden, and it is hard to stop them from coming. Once learned, these responses are extremely resistant to loss.[30]

• Observe how well human beings perform their various activities in what could be described as a kind of trance. They're on automatic pilot. Long-distance driving is performed all the time with the mind elsewhere, yet how efficiently we react to a change in traffic patterns, an unforeseen obstacle. So the tired cellist plays Beethoven flawlessly and without having to think about what he is doing, but he will notice instantly should a string go ever so slightly out of tune.[31]

• The activation of mental networks in the retrieval process can result in a tangible sensation, the feeling of knowing. An acute form of this is the tip-of-the-tongue phenomena, often accompanied by an awareness of the first letter of the word sought or the possession of a word similar to it. The feeling can be likened to a sneeze, a feeling of being on the brink, mildly uncomfortable, followed by considerable relief when the word pops into one's mind.[32]

• Memory is hard put to recreate smells, although nothing evokes a past event so strongly as a smell that was associated with it. Most people can identify fewer than half the odors presented to them in laboratory experiments because of our limited ability to conjure up odors in our mind and our weak association between odors and names. The feeling, "What is that smell? I know it well," is similar to the tip-of-the-tongue phenomenon but differs in that the subject has no clues such as the first letter or general configuration of the word. In this case it is called, of course, the tip-of-the-nose phenomenon.[33]

• Eidetic memory, known better as photographic memory, is more common in young children and often fades as concepts and symbols replace visual perceptions. It is characterized by, for example, the ability to recall exactly the pages of a book. It is really the persistence of especially strong imagery over time.[34]

• Consider the Shass Pollak. He has committed to memory the entire contents of the Talmud. If a page is chosen at random from the thousands of pages of text, the Shass Pollak, given the page number, can identify the fourth word in line twenty-three, for example, or any word anywhere on the page. It is as if his brain has photographed the pages. This is purely eidetic memory. There is no evidence that content has great significance to the Shass Pollak or that he is given to scholarly interpretation of the text. Such extraordinary feats of memory may exist in disproportion to other powers, even to the point of stunting them.[35]

• The other side of rote memory is memory for meaning. The actual words are lost. From an evolutionary standpoint this kind of learning is much more desirable. Language is probably translated from STM to LTM in a recoded shorthand that captures the gist. Fortunately, human beings have a much better memory for gist than for the exact words used to transmit a thought.[36]

• Iconic memory. Close your eyes after looking at an unusually vivid and colorful image and the image remains briefly in your head. The moving tip of a lit cigarette in a dark room makes a trace in the air that lingers afterward.

• *Déjà vu* (literally, already seen) has two contradictory aspects. There is the strong feeling that an event has happened before; at the same time we are quite sure it hasn't. A place where one has never been before may suddenly seem strongly familiar. We think we are remembering what are actually new experiences. Such episodes last only a minute or two and are infrequent. Their cause is not fully understood.[37]

Here's how Dickens described déjà vu in *David Copperfield:* "Copperfield suddenly experienced the illusory recognition, which he described with an almost scientific exactitude as follows: 'We have all some experience of a feeling, that comes over us occasionally, of what we are saying and doing having been said before and done before, in a remote time—of our having been surrounded dim ages ago, by the same faces, objects and circumstances—or our knowing perfectly what will be said next, as if we suddenly remembered it!'"

• Flashbulb memories are vivid memories of a particularly dramatic scene or event in which we had some participation. They tend to be of short duration and have great clarity. An especially forceful form of episodic memory, they are interesting because they are about the person experiencing the memory, not the memory itself. (Do you remember your reaction and where you were when you heard that President Kennedy had been shot?)[38]

• Some people with low I.Q.s have amazing memories for numbers and can perform prodigious mathematical calculations even though they can neither read nor write. They are called *idiots savants*. About one in every two thousand retarded people shows an extraordinary talent, usually for mathematics, art, or music.[39]

• Prosopagnosia is a rare brain disorder. After encephalitis or stroke, victims of this disorder cannot recognize faces, even their own. They can compensate by adopting devices for identifying people. (For example, my husband parts his hair in the middle; that man with his hair parted in the middle must therefore be my husband.) Often victims of prosopagnosia cannot distinguish between a tuxedo and a running suit; all dogs look alike, as do all cats, including lions and kittens.[40]

EYEWITNESS REPORTING
Memory as evidence

It's not as infallible as it sounds.

We can relive events that happened a long time ago. We can see clearly in our mind's eye a scene from the past. This kind of recall happens all the time and gives us the illusion that we are remembering a past event precisely. We aren't. Tape recorders and movie cameras duplicate, people recreate a version of what happened. Memory is selective.[41]

However much we pride ourselves on the accuracy of our recall of a certain set of events, it is nearly impossible for us to distinguish between what we literally remember and what we reconstruct. We fill in the interstices in our memory with our imagination. We fill in with things that are logically and emotionally acceptable. Memory is malleable, subject to distortion. With certain kinds of interference it can be quite transformed. So it is that we can make reconstructions of past experiences that bear, in fact, no relation to the truth. They are fanciful guesses. To further cloud the issue, the level of confidence the witness has that he or she remembers correctly bears absolutely no relationship to the degree of accuracy of the report.

In an experiment, a woman walks into a college classroom and says that she has lost her wallet. She remains in the room about twenty seconds. At the end of the class the students are shown twelve photographs and are encouraged to identify the woman from among them. All do so. However, the woman's picture is not among the photographs; therefore all make wrong choices. Several days later the students are shown another selection of photographs

Notice the objects in the boxes.

including one of the woman and their original wrong choices. Now 22 percent make the correct choice, 44 percent choose their original photograph, and 34 percent choose another one.

How far can you lead people? In trying to get at the facts surrounding a car accident, witnesses are asked, "Did you see a broken headlight?" and, "Did you see the broken headlight?" (No headlight was broken.) Many more witnesses respond positively to the second phrasing than to the first. The witness creates broken glass in his mind. Words like *smashed, hit, collided* evoke worse disasters in memory than *bumped* or *made contact with.* The recollection of the witness has been actually altered by the leading question. We are very suggestible.

What factors influence the accuracy of eyewitness reporting? Delay in reporting causes distortion, as does stress, as does exposure of the witness to other versions of the event. A medium level of stress improves memory, but a lot or a little impairs it. But people are stressed in different ways, and one person's stress may be another's stimulation. There is no clear answer and no scientific basis for assessing the influence of stress on the accuracy of eyewitness accounts.

The Yerkes-Dodson Curve indicates that at high levels of 'stress memory performance declines.

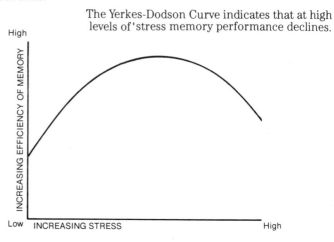

High

INCREASING EFFICIENCY OF MEMORY

Low   INCREASING STRESS   High

All of this has an obvious impact on the use of eyewitness testimony in civil and criminal law cases. It is very hard to shake the impression left by confident eyewitness testimony. Why does a jury prefer to believe the eyewitness rather than the alibi witness? We don't know why, but the fact is, it does. Lenell Jeter spent sixteen months in jail because a woman positively (and incorrectly) identified him as the man who robbed a Kentucky Fried Chicken stand. It took the airing of his story on *Sixty Minutes* and in a Dallas newspaper to reopen his case and eventually get him acquitted. Though he has a lifetime supply of fried chicken by way of apology, Jeter most likely would have preferred to skip the whole experience.

A man hears what he wants to hear and disregards the rest.

— Simon and Garfunkel "The Boxer"

If you are the defense attorney how do you shake strong and compelling evidence? That's where psychologists (expert witnesses, expert testimony) come in. A relatively new phenomenon, the use of expert witnesses has arisen partly in response to the impact made by a confident witness who may be wrong.

There are three ways to question a witness: (1) the police method—"Tell us everything you can remember"; (2) the guided interview—recalling the context, weather, emotions, perspective, etc.; and (3) hypnosis. Contrary to previous findings, we know now that hypnosis doesn't distort. Yet people can flat out lie under hypnosis—worse, they may try to please the interviewer. The guided interview is the best technique. People can report an event differently because their cognitive environments at the time of encoding were different. Two people may interpret the same event differently. Episodic memory is much more subject to loss or alteration than semantic memory.

Training people to be better witnesses doesn't work. Extreme fright may cause amnesia, not only for the event but for what preceded it. Known as retrograde amnesia, it is often triggered by a violent event. After a terrible incident people need to forget, just as they need to find a scapegoat after a catastrophe. Memory tries to provide one.[42]

OTHER VOICES, OTHER ROOMS

Forgetting and Not Forgetting

Much is forgotten. This is both useful and necessary. Forgetting helps us to survive tragedy. The memory of physical pain fades rapidly: we remember that it was unpleasant, that it hurt, but then we move on. Troubled children who grow into contented adults are able to do so in part because they have fewer memories of their painful childhoods than do those who continue to suffer from emotional problems. The former can fashion their memories to fit their current image of themselves.[43]

On the whole, human beings are more likely to remember pleasant things. Tests of childhood memories show that 50 percent are pleasant, 30 percent unpleasant, and 20 percent neutral.[44] Do we repress unpleasant things, or in fact do more good than bad things happen to us? Freud, in *The Psychopathology of Everyday Life*, said that we refuse to remember, that we repress and exclude unacceptable thoughts. But sometimes nothing imprints memories more strongly than the desire to forget. And, of course, many things we think are gone are not gone at all but can be retrieved by drugs, psychiatry, electrical stimulation, or some other strong stimulus, and suddenly, there they are. The past is powerful. Or as William Faulkner put it: "The past is not dead, it is not even past."

Without the ability to forget, the mind would be cluttered with endless trivia. Is this happening to us culturally? Are we overwhelmed with information? Consider the Russian mnemonist Shereshevskii. There was no limit to what he could remember: long lists of nonsense syllables, hundred-digit numbers, a table of four hundred numbers arranged at random in a twenty by twenty grid pattern, poetry in languages he did not speak. He could recite all these things backwards as well as forwards and do it equally well many years after learning them. He had synesthesia, the ability to create a wealth of images and to code information in several sensory ways. Words were puffs of steam or splashes, certain sounds were velvet cords or had a sweet or sour taste.[45] Some of us have this capacity to a lesser degree in that we think, as Shereshevskii did, of days of the week as colors, of numbers as resembling people, of high-pitched sounds as having an abrasive texture.

Shereshevskii was very successful on stage with his amazing memory, but his mind created so many images that they got in each other's way. The result was chaos. He needed to do some forgetting. Fortunately he was able to think of his mind as a blackboard that he could erase when necessary. He could image a white object against a white background and thus make it vanish, or he could put something in a dark place and lose it. Sometimes he wrote what he wanted to forget on a piece of paper and tore it up.[46] Most of us don't have this much trouble forgetting. We can use imaging techniques instead to help us remember.

Why do we forget? Perhaps some synapses just shut off temporarily. Possibly the memory trace fades away. Possibly the trace is overlaid with interference, obscured by subsequent information. The more similar the interfering material, the greater the forgetting.[47] Then there is the old problem of paying insufficient attention in the first place. Arousal improves memory performance; boredom, preoccupation, and depression interfere with it. But too much arousal—as in anxiety, stress, or fear—interferes with performance, too.

There is a pathological forgetting called "fugue," literally, "flight." An extended episode of acting as a different person, fugue is more common in time of war, but can happen at any time. It's one way human beings may deal with acute and unresolved conflict. People whose lives have become intolerable can, in effect, cease to be themselves temporarily as a means of fending off anxiety. They don't forget how to function, write, speak, drive a car, etc.; they forget what makes them themselves. When they return to their normal state, often spontaneously, they can remember nothing of the episode through which they have passed. Fugue is precipitated by an intense conflict or an emotional crisis. It is not well understood, and is by no means common.[48]

An obvious but trusty bulwark against everyday forgetfulness is to be organized, to structure one's life, having backup reminder systems for what is really important. Yet we must lose some of the information with which we are constantly bombarded in order to function, in order to retain our sanity. A condition of remembering is that we should forget.

If you should forget me for a while
And afterwards remember, do not grieve:
. . . .
Better by far you should forget and smile
Than that you should remember and be sad.
                              — Christina Rossetti
                              "Remember"

VARIETIES OF MEMORY LOSS

Aging

The self-centered western emphasis on the importance of the individual makes old age seem an outrage and an affront rather than a logical and necessary part of the process of living. Measuring human worth in terms of productivity, as our fast-paced society seems to do, devalues a long and well-lived life when it ceases to be as productive as it was in its prime. Some of us comply in our own devaluation, experience feelings of worthlessness, cease to be proud of our many accomplishments, fail to adjust to inevitable changes and losses. Old people, too, can adapt and thrive, though their ability to do so depends on their personalities, health, life experiences, and the support they receive from society. Dr. Robert N. Butler writes, "Failure of adaptation at any age under any circumstances can result in a physical or emotional illness. Optimal growth and adaptation may occur all along the course of life when the individual's strengths and potentials are recognized, reinforced and encouraged by the environment in which he lives."

The notion that old people inevitably become senile, show forgetfulness, have episodes of confusion and reduced attention is simply wrong. Like "crazy," the word "senile" is no longer acceptable; it isn't a medical term, and it has no agreed-upon meaning. It is loosely used to describe changes in later life, especially memory changes. But memory changes can be temporary, triggered by bereavement, anxiety, or any stressful situation that makes it hard to concentrate. These changes are treatable and reversible.[49]

Everyone begins to lose memory at about age twenty. Vocabulary and knowledge continue to increase, but our ability to learn and learn rapidly peaks at an early age. If people in their thirties lose their car keys or wallet, or call one child by the name of another, no one gives it a second thought. We have all found ourselves in the basement with no recollection of what we meant to find or do there. When a seventy-year-old does these things, concern is unjustifiable. The fact is that people who stay intellectually alive can expect their minds to stay clear throughout their lives.

And yet, not all minds do. An aging population is at risk for the diseases of aging; some memory loss is normal or benign and some is not. Memory loss can be an early symptom of a dementing disease, in particular the disease called Alzheimer's, first documented as a brain disease by Alois Alzheimer, a German psychologist, in 1906.

The incidence of Alzheimer's disease has increased enormously in recent years. Why? Is it because people are living longer? Or is the disease simply better documented now? Are environmental toxins responsible? Immunologic changes? A slow virus? We don't quite know yet. Fifteen years ago Alzheimer's was poorly documented and little talked about. Now it is the subject of intensive scientific investigation. Now we give rapt attention to any breakthrough in the management of this disease that so relentlessly alters the lives it touches.

Two men are walking on a beach in Florida.
First man: Good morning, I'm Ernest Scott. What's your
   name?
Second man: How soon do you need to know?

Alzheimer's Disease

Dementia is not a nice or pleasant word, especially when applied to people we love. The *Journal of the Royal College of Physicians* offers the following definition: "Dementia is the global impairment of higher cortical function including memory, the capacity to solve problems of day-to-day living, the performance of learned perceptor-motor skills, the correct use of social skills and control of emotional reactions, in the absence of gross clouding of consciousness. The condition is often irreversible and progressive."

The victim of Alzheimer's exhibits inappropriate emotional reactions. These people can't do the simple, everyday tasks they used to do, and they lack judgment. There is no metabolic abnormality and no impairment—even in the late stages—of the ability to think. It's just that dementia patients cannot think clearly, logically, or by our definition, rationally. They are often obsessive. In fact, they are really no longer the people we once knew. The victim feels humiliated, and family and friends acutely feel the sad loss of human potential. It is as if the demented elderly die twice. It has been called the long good-bye.

Alzheimer's (AD) is an age-related illness. It can strike as early as the forties, but usually symptoms begin to appear between fifty-five and sixty-five. According to the Alzheimer's Association, 10% of the population over sixty-five now has Alzheimer's. After eighty-five, 47 percent will have it. Four million Americans have the disease, and this number will more than triple in the next half century. While it accounts for more than half the population of nursing homes today,[50] 70 percent of the care given is provided by families. It costs the nation $90 billion a year, almost all of which is paid by patients and their families. Neither Medicare nor most private health programs pay for the long-term health care required by Alzheimer's patients.

In 1975 the largest population bulge was the age group from eighteen to twenty. In 2025 the group from sixty to eighty will be the largest. By 2050 the United States will have 67.5 million people over sixty-five. Right now the number of Americans over sixty-five exceeds the entire population of Canada. To meet the projected need for nursing homes, forty institutions must be built per month in the next ten years.[51] Need we concern ourselves with these statistics? Yes, indeed. They will have profound political, economic, and medical consequences for everyone.

Alzheimer's is by no means just a memory problem, but the first symptoms are often memory related. Difficulties may first appear with such tasks as keeping a checkbook, paying bills, using a calculator, or consulting maps. Early indications can show up as playing trump inappropriately in card games, repeatedly forgetting major items on a shopping list, or difficulty in cutting meat, tying shoe laces, combing hair. Visual and verbal tasks are performed poorly, and names are readily forgotten.

Abnormalities typical of Alzheimer's include difficulties in learning new skills, in knitting and doing simple needlework, in moving to a new house or going to a shopping center. Adjusting abilities seem virtually nonexistent. Language skills, particularly paraphrasing and understanding speech, are impaired. Familiar tasks become bewildering: one victim cannot remember how a doorknob works. Making coffee is daunting. There are difficulties with motor skills and sometimes with seeing. Visual acuity may show no change, but the person with Alzheimer's may not be able to interpret important visual information and may walk into things. Messages from the retina to the brain can be discombobulated.

These are the symptoms the doctors discuss. What the family sees is different and worse. Loved relatives become hostile strangers. Capable people develop behaviors that require monitoring, as if they were two-year-olds. Incontinence, wandering, aggressive and obsessive behavior bewilder the patient and exhaust the caregiver. A handbook on how to cope with an Alzheimer's patient is called *The Thirty-Six Hour Day.*

So much is still not clear about Alzheimer's. Until recently no reliable diagnostic test was available except brain biopsy, too radical a procedure to be of much use. Most diagnoses were made by autopsy. For the living one had to diagnose by elimination. Other dementia-producing factors had to be ruled out: blows to the head, stroke, lesion, tumor, depression, adverse drug reaction, thyroid problems. When there is a progressive erosion of mental function and nothing else left to consider, then it must be Alzheimer's.

Computerized tomography (CAT scan) and SPECT scan reveal brain activity. In a PET scan, radioactive glucose injected into the brain can be followed by the scanner as it is absorbed. Diseased or dying areas do not absorb the glucose and appear dark blue. More accessible as a diagnostic tool is magnetic resonance imaging (MRI), a technique capable of generating precise images of the brain. But these procedures, too, diagnose by eliminating other factors.

A key protein has been identified in the spinal fluid and in the blood of Alzheimer's patients. A test for the presence

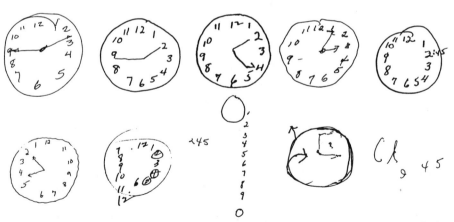

Ten Alzheimer's patients were told, "Please draw a clock. Put the hands on the clock to read 2:45." *Research of Trey Sunderland, M.D. and colleagues at the National Institute of Mental Health. Reprinted with permission.*

of this protein is close to being ready. Until it is, neuropsychological tests remain the principal method of diagnosis. These tests for memory, communication skills, and activities of daily living are specific to Alzheimer's.

Seen under a microscope, the brains of those who have died of Alzheimer's show plaques and tangles—curious blotches composed of a central core of protein wrapped in knots of fibers that have sprouted and snarled. For decades scientists have puzzled over the causes of these anatomical hallmarks of the disease. Recent studies indicate that a protein called beta-amyloid may undergo a chemical alteration that renders it damaging to the nerve cells. It remains to locate where the abnormal processing occurs, and then to block it. Sound simple? It isn't. But both biochemical and genetic evidence point to the amyloid protein as a culprit in nerve cell loss. According to Donald Price, a neurologist and pathologist at Johns Hopkins University, it is not known why normal proteins break down. "We have the molecular players in the right ballpark, at least, but we don't know the rules of the game."[52]

Diagnosis is essential for the 15 percent of dementias that are treatable. For Alzheimer's there really isn't any

HEALTHY BRAIN   ALZHEIMER'S BRAIN

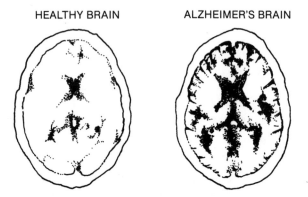

Computer imaging techniques reveal the extent of brain damage, the erosion of the cortical rim, in Alzheimer's disease.

good news yet about how to prevent the disease or how to ameliorate its ravages once they appear. Cross-sections of the affected brain show that the cortical rim, the gray matter, is gone. Acetylcholine, a chemical that is important in the transmission of nerve impulses, is decreased. Scientists at the National Institute of Mental Health are attempting to develop drugs that supplement acetylcholine, but research is still far from providing a treatment.[53]

Breakthroughs have been made. A gene that appears to be associated with the tangles and plaques has been identified. The gene is located on the same chromosome that is involved in Down's syndrome (mongolism), a form of mental retardation that is apparent in infancy. While there is some genetic link or family predisposition, more than 90 percent of Alzheimer's cases have no familial connection.

Aluminum, once thought to be a culprit because accumulations of it are found in the tangled nerve cells of AD brains, has been largely exonerated. Aluminum is an abundant metallic element, and it is no more likely a cause of Alzheimer's than a consequence of it.

The Alzheimer's Association, with its more than two hundred chapters and sixteen hundred support groups,

---

Some helpful books on Alzheimer's Disease:

The Thirty-Six Hour Day, by Nancy L. Mace and Dr. Peter V. Rabins (Warner, pbk., 1989)

The Loss of Self, by Drs. Donna Cohen and Carl Eisdorfer (New American Library, pbk., 1987)

When Your Loved One Has Alzheimer's, by David Carroll (HarperCollins, pbk., 1989)

Coping with Alzheimer's: A Caregiver's Emotional Survival Guide, by Rose Oliver and Francis Bock (Wilshire, pbk., 1989)

For twenty-four-hour information and referral, contact the Alzheimer's Association, 919 North Michigan Avenue, Chicago, IL 60611-1676. Telephone: 1-800-272-3900.

provides a clearing house for information and referral. A support group, or just someone at the other end of the phone who understands, helps alleviate the caregiver's isolation and devastation. The burden of continual care stretches resources beyond their limits. Feelings of guilt and being overwhelmed are common; talking with others who have dealt with the same problem is a great source of relief. And finally the need for respite care, time-out for the caregiver, is receiving national attention.

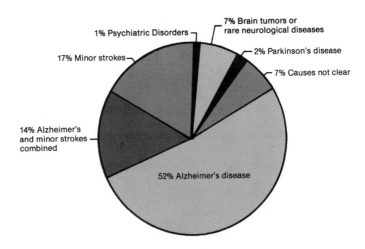

Current research indicates that about half of the dementias that affect older people are caused by Alzheimer's.

Korsakoff's Psychosis

Memory disorders, a variety of impairments, offer clues to brain function. The study of how memory breaks down, how cognition fails, helps scientists learn about the nature and organization of normal memory. Like a machine, memory can be manipulated and its behavior observed. Research pits one type of cognitive operation against another, one type of drug against another, and does this in contrasting groups of patients. By testing drugs, people, and processes, scientists begin to have a framework for answering some of the questions. Some drugs affect episodic memory and some semantic memory, just as some forms of amnesia affect one kind of memory and not another.

Korsakoff's psychosis, a brain syndrome of alcoholism, includes a selective memory failure often studied by psychologists. The chronic undernourishment, especially thiamine deficiency, that often accompanies alcoholism, causes certain areas of the brain to disintegrate. While many functions of the brain remain intact, certain aspects of memory are impaired. Korsakoff's patients have a kind of pure amnesia in which the contents of short-term memory are not transferred into permanent storage.

Korsakoff's psychosis is the result of structural damage to the brain; it is irreversible. Superficially, victims appear demented in ways similar to Alzheimer's patients, but there are differences. Korsakoff's victims use clever strategies for hiding memory failure. They have a large repertoire of socially acceptable responses that mask the fact that they don't know the answer. They confabulate; they make up an appropriate story and tell it in a jovial way; but the story is not based on fact. They don't know what day it is, and they don't care. They have no information to transmit, they cannot learn new things; their trusty old social sense continues to work well for them, but it is no longer based on reality.[54]

In research, patients with Korsakoff's psychosis are compared in various aspects of cognition with Parkinson's patients, with patients who have undergone electroconvulsive therapy (ECT), with Alzheimer's patients and with normal volunteers. What can be learned from these comparisons?

Briefly, those with Korsakoff's psychosis are impaired in recent memory. With them it is last in, first out. They may well know what happened in 1940, but not what happened last week. They are badly impaired on tests involving sequence and order. This would indicate a dissociation between semantic (knowledge) memory and episodic (personal) memory. Another example: these patients are good at solving complicated puzzles and can perform equally well months later, even though they have no conscious memory of the procedure or of the puzzles.

On the other hand, patients with Alzheimer's have access to old knowledge and can also often remember recent events. But they have a great deal of trouble completing a sentence such as, "We worked all morning and then took a break for _____." An Alzheimer's brain has impoverished structures. Where once there were many elements and bridges between structures, now both the elements and the relationships have begun to erode. Ask someone with Alzheimer's disease to name all the birds and you will get the sparrows and pigeons, but the herons are gone. The structure hasn't disappeared, but it is less elaborated. This erosion of knowledge memory makes puzzle-solving virtually impossible.[55]

Amnesia

Remember reading stories in which, after a fight, the hero didn't remember anything until another blow on the head brought it all back and resolved everything? Amnesia isn't really like that. It can be much more selective and a lot less charming. It gives us another window on how we remember and why we forget.

The causes of amnesia are: dementia (Alzheimer's disease, Parkinson's disease, and others), head injury, Korsakoff's psychosis, stroke, viral encephalitis (herpes simplex), ruptured aneurysm, anoxia (cardiac arrest, near drowning, carbon monoxide poisoning), and electroconvulsive therapy.

There are two components to the memory impairment seen in amnesics. One is anterograde amnesia—the inability to learn new material from the day of the amnesia forward. The other is retrograde amnesia—loss of memory or inability to get at the information that was stored normally before the onset of amnesia. Although taking away the past does damage to the personality and sense of selfhood, the inability to form new memories is far more disabling, says Richard Restak in *The Brain.*

Electroconvulsive therapy (ECT), given for serious depression, is instructive for the student of amnesia in that it acts as its own control. It is a scheduled event, and the patient enters the hospital with a normal memory. Immediately following each treatment there is a temporary and reversible amnesia. During the fifteen minutes or so after treatment, the subject can neither get access to memories of the last few years nor store what's happening during the fifteen minutes. ECT is given typically three times a week for three to five weeks. By the fifth treatment its effects last considerably longer, and by the tenth treatment longer still. Several months later memory for events preceding treatments returns, except possibly for the period immediately before each treatment, but memory for events during and immediately after each treatment will never return. ECT causes both anterograde and retrograde amnesia for the time spent in the hospital during and immediately after each treatment.

The memory system fractionates or breaks apart at the seams in patients with amnesia. The types of damage suffered are highly specific; they affect particular processes while leaving other processes intact.

Childhood Amnesia

Childhood amnesia is a sinister-sounding label for our failure to remember our earliest experiences. Memories of fetal experiences and those of infancy and earliest childhood simply do not exist or are not accessible. Considering the richness of our early years, it's surprising that we have so few memories of them. Why? And when does memory begin?

Freud was wont to blame the blanks in our babyhood on repression of feelings of aggression or sexuality, all the things we couldn't deal with. It may be much simpler than that. Perhaps very young children don't have an autobiographical memory yet, or sufficiently sophisticated structures for storing their experiences. Before age three or so human beings don't have any time sense, don't have much self-reference, and don't use the past tense well. Young children refer to everything in the past as yesterday. Swiss child psychologist Jean Piaget points out that children report confusion, that in their earliest memories events are not in any order. Typically the first memory is like a snapshot, still and crisp, a frozen visual image.[56]

Many think that memory begins with the acquisition of language, which depends on semantic memory. Semantic or general knowledge memory develops before episodic or autobiographical memory. Children do have some semantic memory, even if it's not well developed, but episodic memory isn't there yet. Episodic events of childhood do not enter directly into memory. Others tell us about them until they become part of our semantic memory. From there they pass into episodic memory and autobiographical memory begins. With episodic memory you have a strong feeling that you were there. Thus childhood memories—real or imagined—have significant diagnostic value because of what they tell us about our attitudes toward ourselves, others, life.[57] Our often powerful motivation to remember and understand our childhood is part of the search for identity. Our obsession with identity is a relatively recent phenomenon.

We have many more neurons at birth than we do as

adults. Probably a lot of early information has to be discarded because it can't be stored. Or possibly it's stored, but we can't retrieve it. Psychologists don't talk about things that are forgotten anymore; they talk about things that can't be retrieved. The names of your first-grade classmates must be in there even though you can't get at them. Can you?

Many children's games are pure memory tests:

"I Packed My Grandmother's Trunk" consists of two or more players verbally putting various items, tangible and intangible, into granny's trunk, taking turns and listing all the previous items in order. Usually played alphabetically and not too difficult, it becomes much more difficult when played with no such aide-memoire.

"Concentration," or "Memory," calls for placing one or more decks of cards face down on a table. The object is to accumulate pairs by remembering the cards each player turns up, locating them, and pairing them up when your turn comes. Victory goes to the player who most consistently remembers the location of unpaired cards previously turned. This game, too, becomes more difficult when the cards are not put in orderly rows, but set out at random.

Such games probably sharpen concentration—and memory—at any age.

SOME INTERESTING CASE HISTORIES

The most famous amnesic patient is H.M. Subject to many epileptic seizures daily, he underwent drastic brain surgery in 1953 at age twenty-seven. The procedure included bilateral removal of structures including the amygdala and the hippocampus. As a result he has a profound inability to learn new information about the world: he cannot store new memories. He is grossly impaired for learning new words. He does not know his age, the date, where he lives; he does not know his recent history or the status of his mother and father. Both parents are deceased, and H.M. grieves as at a fresh sorrow each time he is told of their deaths. He looks at a picture of himself and thinks it is his father. He is stuck at the age at which he had surgery.

H.M. can't keep track of time at all. He can eat lunch all over again, not remembering having eaten it. Normal conversation is difficult because he has no content, no chitchat. When he talks he sounds fine. His intellectual and perceptual abilities are fine; he does well on IQ tests. Except for his amnesia, he is really quite intact. He is aware of his disability. He engages in perfectly normal conversation so long as the person he is talking with provides the input. But if the conversation stops and the other person walks away and comes back, H.M. doesn't remember what was talked about or that there was a conversation and doesn't remember the other person. This is anterograde amnesia, the inability to store new facts. In addition, H.M. has retrograde amnesia for the period from his sixteenth to his twenty-seventh year. He is grossly impaired for that period even though his memory for the period before that is intact. In retrograde amnesia what is learned earliest is intact. Last in, first out is a general rule of thumb for memory loss.

The operation performed on H.M. has not been performed since.

In 1985 J., a fifty-five-year-old man, was under considerable stress and having problems at work. One day his wife and two teenage children came home to find him sitting on the floor in the kitchen with the heating element from the electric oven in his hand. He had a glazed expression on his face and was completely unresponsive.

In a day or two he had recovered somewhat but still did not recognize his wife and children. He thought it was 1945, that he was fourteen, and that he was in the hospital because he had been hit on the head with a baseball bat. Such an accident had, in fact, occurred when he was fourteen, though no one remembers it as a particularly serious incident. That time was, however, easily the happiest period of his life. Today, he is still stuck at age fourteen. After the critical event that left him dazed on the kitchen floor, he was amazed at the snappy car he had bought his wife (and at the existence of his wife), the stereo and VCR, the microwave, none of which he knew how to work.

J. has undergone a profound loss. He has lost his memory for events; he knows nothing of his life since 1945. His vocabulary and knowledge of the world are those of a fourteen-year-old. He doesn't know words that have come into the language since 1945. His skills have rolled back: he plays tennis and golf like a boy, even though as a man he was quite proficient. His handwriting has become very deliberate. His accent has become as southern as it was at age fourteen. He can't believe that his face requires shaving and that his hair is thinning. He knows intellectually what everyone tells him, but he can't quite accept it. He acts like a very immature boy, is nervous around girls, giggles, and slides down banisters in shopping malls.

What is amazing about J. is the selectivity of his forgetting. You and I couldn't do it—we couldn't remember only the things we learned before a certain date and lose the rest. What happened to him? Possibly his memory was normal until 1985 and then something happened. Or perhaps the way his brain stored information acquired since 1945 was different. The best bet is that his problem is psychogenic, that his loss of memory is a defense mechanism that permits him to go back to a happier time.

In standard amnesias that have both a retrograde and an anterograde component, procedural memory—the memory for skills—is preserved. But J. has retrograde amnesia for all memory systems, including procedural memory. J. does not have anterograde amnesia; he can learn new things—how to drive a car and work appliances—but H.M. can't. There are many variations among amnesias. What does this say about the structure of memory? Certainly it tells us that amnesia affects some systems and not others, that memory is indeed not one but many systems.

Amnesic patients do retain some learning abilities. They can perform a task over a period of time and improve consistently, but they can't remember having done the task before. They can learn skills, even though they can't learn someone's name.[58]

I find that the further back I go, the better I remember things, whether they happened or not.

— Mark Twain

THE STATE OF THE RESEARCH
Help May Be on the Way

But it isn't here yet. There are no medicines to reverse dementia or to restore memory once it's gone. The splash of a newscast touting a breakthrough in the treatment of memory loss is followed in a few days by more sober news. We don't know why certain drugs do what they do, or how they can be used most effectively in the fight against dementia. Alzheimer's is a failure of several systems; one medication won't be the answer. The state of the research is similar to the state of cancer research in the 1950s.

The average thirty-five-year-old American takes four to five pills a day, including vitamins. A sixty-five-year-old American may take twenty pills a day. Nursing home patients may take sixty pills a day. The effects of drugs on old people may be quite different from their effects on younger men and women. Tranquilizers and sleeping pills often have temporary memory-impairing effects that last longer in older people or those unaccustomed to medication. Sometimes memory can be magically restored if the medicine is stopped.[59]

The disciplines studying these ambiguous areas of memory and brain function are beginning to interact. The psychobiology of cognition and cognitive failure crisscrosses neuroanatomy, neuropsychology, neuropharmacology, and cognitive psychology.

A revolution in the understanding of brain chemistry began in the 1960s. The brain was found to have natural receptors for certain opiates; from them the existence of natural substances with opiate-like properties was inferred.

This was a great step forward in the study and development of drugs to act on these highly specialized systems.[60]

New techniques in genetic engineering and molecular biology are leading away from the use of chemotherapeutic drugs to the use of biological substances. Doctors will be able to manipulate the patient's own network of biochemical balances and defenses to combat illness.[61]

Alzheimer's victims show a deficiency in a number of brain chemicals, notably the neurotransmitters that affect mood, memory, coordination, energy, and reflexes. The process by which these substances are broken down, a process that increases with normal aging, increases dramatically in Alzheimer's sufferers.

In patients with certain memory disorders, supplementing choline, which stimulates production of the neurotransmitter acetylcholine, can sometimes reduce or slow symptoms of Alzheimer's, even if it cannot restore the deterioration. Choline is found in the food substance lecithin, which is present in egg yolks and soybeans. To be effective, however, lecithin has to be taken in a pure form. There is little evidence that general memory performance can be enhanced by food supplements.[62]

When tacrine, otherwise known as THA (for tetrahydroaminoacridine), came on the market it was hailed as a wonder drug. It appears to be able to raise the level of acetylcholine, and some Alzheimer's patients who were given it did indeed show improvement. However, after review by a Food and Drug Administration advisory panel, it was decided that the drug didn't "show a clinically meaningful benefit" and that it carried a significant risk of liver damage. It was taken off the market.

Every drug has more than one effect, some known, some unknown, some desirable, some undesirable. Public speakers who take tranquilizers to allay stage fright might try other tactics if they knew that these medications actually impair memory.

Certain drugs improve memory for a period of several weeks. Vasopressin, a chemical found in the brain, is associated with memory, thirst, rage, addiction, fear, and pain. Still in the experimental stages as a kidney drug, it has some dangerous side effects on the body's circulation and water retention. But vasopressin in drug form enhances memory, sometimes dramatically, with effects that last about three weeks. How many questions does this raise for the future? Will we have lazy students popping vasopressin? Will users find themselves inundated by memories to the point of incoherence, overwhelmed by memories like Shereshev-skii? Will those things we have tried so hard to put out of our minds come flooding back? As Richard Restak suggests, not everyone may want to remember. Some people may say "thanks, but no thanks" to memories of childhood poverty or indifference, of unhappy marriages, of disappointments or missed opportunities.

There is enough compelling evidence that drugs can affect memory to have drug companies scrambling to be first with a workable memory enhancer. But so far no drug is free from side effects, and the laboratory isn't the world. There is no memory pill ready for the world.

IN CONCLUSION
Resist PWELGAS

By the time we are adults we have lost half our synaptic connections and our brains have shrunk. A reduced blood flow is sending less oxygen to fewer synapses in a diminished brain.

But cheer up, things really aren't so bad. We still have many synapses left, and we aren't doing all that badly. Even though we forget some people's names, think how many we remember. It's all right to forget some of the names of the people at the cocktail party, as long as you don't forget the whole party.

Read aloud, speak aloud, write things down. Most information comes through seeing; use the other senses to reinforce it. Remember things in sequence, in categories, in relationships. Use association, linking, imaging. Use all five senses. Be organized. Pay attention. Best of all, be interested.

Distribute practice. For better learning, study a little each day. Study, then take a break, and repeat this process. Don't study for long, uninterrupted hours. We remember better if we make ourselves recall material rather than reread it. Use effortful memory; the search process actually helps imprint the information.

Remember that a lot of everyday memory lapses are merely interruptions of the search sequence, the result of external interference breaking our concentration.

The less that happens between learning and recall, the better. Avoid proactive interference (a major distraction during the learning process) and retroactive interference (a hurricane or earthquake immediately after learning).[63]

It is six times more efficient to memorize or learn something at night; sleep seems to act as a fixative. There is

9 percent retention eight hours later of things learned before noon, and 56 percent retention of things learned just before bedtime.[64] Short-term memory is more effective in the morning, but long-term memory is more efficient at night because of the normally higher state of arousal in the evening.[65] There is little evidence that playing tapes of material to learn while asleep is effective.

Though college students may be better at rote memorization and quicker in general, they are not at all more efficient in life than older people. Adults learn to take advantage of memory aids such as diaries, appointment calendars, and lists. They tend to be better organized, which more than compensates for the speed of youth.

Memory aids such as acronyms, rhymes, first letter sentences, deliberately putting something in the wrong place, even cooking timers, any and all mnemonic devices—don't underestimate them. "Thirty days hath September" has been helping people remember the number of days in the month since the sixteenth century. "If the face is red raise the head, if the face is pale raise the tail" is handy first-aid advice. How about NATO, MADD, CREEP, FACE, and ROY G. BIV, Every Good Boy Does Fine, and Rats Have Yellow Top Hats, Mama? Can you identify the only place in the United States where four states touch? UCAN. How about the planets in order away from the sun? My Very Earnest Mother Just Served Us Nine Pickles. Which side do you leave a buoy on coming into a harbor? Red Right Returning. Stubborn screws? Try rightsy tightsy, lefty loosey. Need to remember the seven hills of Rome? Poor Queen Victoria Eats Crow At Christmas. How about the sides in the War of the Roses? Think *White* Plains, New *York*. Exceptions to the rule? Neither leisured foreigner seized the weird heights. Spring forward, fall back. Above all shun PWELGAS.*

One more memory tip. For the remembering of names, which for many of us seem to disappear relentlessly into a black hole: pay attention, of course, say the name aloud and then get a handle on it, hook it to something, give it a context. For instance, when you meet Mr. Karnoussian, picture his car hanging from a tree in a noose. Make it a Silver Shadow Rolls Royce, if you like. Mrs. Hatfield is a field full of hats. Miss Bellinger becomes a bellringer: have her swinging from the clapper in your mind—the more vivid, the more arresting the image, the better for remembering. It gets your attention. This technique applies to remembering anything: associate something new with something already known, and then imprint it, use imagination to make it memorable.

When all else fails, have diversionary and coping skills at the ready. No one will notice or remember that you forgot.[66]

> "The horror of that moment," the King
> went on, "I shall never, never forget."
> "You will though," the Queen said, "if
> you don't make a memorandum of it."
> — Lewis Carroll
> *Through the Looking Glass*

* North Atlantic Treaty Organization, Mothers Against Drunk Driving, Committee to Re-Elect the President, in music the notes between the treble staff lines, the colors in the spectrum: red, orange, yellow, green, blue, indigo, violet; the notes on the treble staff lines; the correct spelling of rhythm; Utah, Colorado, Arizona, New Mexico; Mercury, Venus, Earth, Mars, Jupiter, Saturn, Uranus, Neptune, Pluto; Palatine, Quirinal, Viminal, Esquiline, Capolitine, Avetine, Caelian; the white rose was the emblem of the House of York, as the red rose was of the House of Lancaster; exceptions to the rule 'i' before 'e' except after 'c' unless sounded like 'a' as in 'neighbor' and 'weigh'; how to adjust your clocks to Daylight or Standard Time; the seven deadly sins: Pride, Wrath, Envy, Lust, Gluttony, Avarice, Sloth.

Pegwords

Did you notice the ten objects in boxes beginning on page 39? Recall, *in sequence,* as many of them as you can. Five is average, seven is superior, and eight or above is very superior.

"Pegwords" offers a memory system effective for remembering lists of unrelated items in a given order. Learn the following ten words, each one "pegged" to a number and easy to recall because it rhymes: a bun for one, a shoe for two, a tree for three, a door for four, a hive for five, sticks for six, heaven for seven, a gate for eight, wine for nine, and a hen for ten.

Now when confronted with a list of things to remember, imagine the items in relation to the pegwords. If your shopping list reads aspirin, lobster, gas, and stamps, then think, "The aspirin is sitting on a bun, the lobster wears tennis shoes, there's a gas can hanging from the tree, the stamps are sticking to the door," and so forth. Or how about a day of appointments? A client at nine (with a bottle of wine), the doctor at one (the doc has nice buns), a haircut at two (he's forgotten his shoes) . . .

It works. Try it for yourself: go back to the boxed objects in the text and try associating each one, in sequence, with its pegword. Did your score improve?

Memory Survey

Results of a memory survey of some 1,400 adults. Compare yourself with the survey respondents—you will probably be reassured.

How would you describe your ability to remember the following?	Very poor	Poor	About average	Good	Very good
1. The name of a person just introduced to you.	12%	18%	39%	20%	12%
2. Where you have placed objects (such as keys) at home or at the office.	3	8	21	28	39
3. To turn out lights, turn off appliances, and lock doors when leaving home.	2	1	8	23	66
4. Telephone numbers you call once a week or more.	4	7	21	24	43
5. Specific facts from a book, newspaper or magazine article you read one week ago.	4	10	39	29	18
6. Names of teachers and classmates from your early grades of school.	8	16	28	24	24
7. Faces of people you have met only once or twice.	4	16	27	24	29
8. Facts that must be recalled very quickly as in a game or television game show.	4	13	34	27	23
9. Where you parked your car in a shopping center or other congested area.	3	10	19	26	41

How often would you say that you do each of the following?	Very often	Often	Occa-sionally	Rarely	Very rarely
10. Go into a room to get something and forget what you are after.	8	14	38	26	13
11. Arrive at the grocery store or pharmacy and forget what you intended to buy.	5	6	19	36	35
12. Forget that you told someone something and tell that person the same thing again.	7	10	32	31	20
13. Fail to remember a name or word when trying, but recall it later.	9	21	47	17	6
14. Forget an appointment or other event that is very important to you.	2	4	9	33	52
15. Forget items you intended to take with you when traveling.	4	9	25	29	34
16. Forget which waiter took your order in a restaurant.	3	8	20	29	40
17. Forget telephone numbers before they can be dialed.	10	15	25	24	27
18. Store an important item in a place where it will be safe and then forget where it is.	7	15	31	23	24

Notes and Elaborations

1. Information from a lecture given at the Smithsonian Institution by David Horton, Professor of Psychology, University of Maryland.

2. John R. Anderson, *Cognitive Psychology and its Implications* (New York: W. H. Freeman, 1985), 23.

3. Richard Restak, *The Brain* (New York: Bantam Books, 1984), 136–137.

4. Philip J. Hilts, "A Brain Unit Seen as Index for Recalling Memories," *New York Times,* September 24, 1991, C-8.

5. Philip J. Hilts, "Photos Show Mind Recalling a Word," *New York Times,* November 11, 1991, A-11.

6. Sharon Begley, "Thinking Looks Like This," *Newsweek,* November 25, 1991, 67.

7. Sharon Begley, see above.

8. Philip J. Hilts, "Photos Show Mind Recalling a Word," see above.

9. Stanley Burnshaw, *The Seamless Web* (New York: George Braziller, 1978), 69.

10. Anderson, 18.

11. Barry L. Jacobs, "Love as a Neurotransmission," review of *Molecules of the Mind* by Jon Franklin, *New York Times Book Review,* February 8, 1987, 15.

12. Much of this information is from Daniel J. Boorstin, *The Discoverers* (New York: Vintage Books, 1985), 480–488.

13. D. S. Halacy, Jr., *Man and Memory* (New York: Harper & Row, 1978), 8.

14. Boorstin, 488.

15. Richard Bergland, *The Fabric of Mind* (New York: Viking, 1985), 105.

16. Boorstin, 623.

17. Joan Minninger, *Total Recall* (Emmaus, Pa.: Rodale Press, 1984), 63, 75; Restak, 24; Jeremy Campbell, *Winston Churchill's Afternoon Nap* (New York: Simon and Schuster, 1986), 97; Colin Blakemore, *Mechanics of the Mind* (Cambridge: Cambridge University Press, 1977), 102.

18. Restak, 211.

19. Bernard Dixon, "When the Brain Takes the Strain," *New Scientist,* October 23, 1986, 62.

20. Eena Job, *Fending Off Forgetfulness* (St. Lucia, Australia: University of Queensland Press, 1985), 13.

21. Daniel Goleman, "A Conversation with Ulric Neisser," *Psychology Today,* May 1983, 57.

22. Minninger, 93.

23. Jack Smith, *Los Angeles Times,* March 17, 1985, VII, 1.

24. Information from a lecture given at the Smithsonian Institution by Neal Cohen, Associate Professor of Psychology, University of Illinois.

25. Restak, 41.

26. Burnshaw, 2, 14.

27. Colin Blakemore, "The Unsolved Marvel of Memory," *New York Times Magazine,* February 6, 1977, 44.

28. D. S. Halacy, 62.

29. Blakemore, *New York Times Magazine,* 45.

30. Horton lecture.

31. Dixon, 62.

32. Job, 16.

33. Trygg Engen, "Remembering Odors and Their Names," *American Scientist,* September–October 1987, 497–499.

34. D. S. Halacy, 52–54.

35. Ulric Neisser, *Memory Observed: Remembering in Natural Contexts* (San Francisco: W. H. Freeman & Co., 1982), 312.

36. E. D. Hirsch, Jr., *Cultural Literacy: What Every American Needs to Know* (Boston: Houghton Mifflin, 1987), 36.

37. I. M. L. Hunter, *Memory* (Baltimore: Penguin Books, 1974), 39.

38. David C. Rubin, "The Subtle Deceiver: Recalling our Past," *Psychology Today,* September 1985, 39.

39. Minninger, 130.

40. Sandra Blakeslee, "Memory Disorders Seen as Clue to Brain's Function," *New York Times,* June 14, 1985, A-16.

41. Hunter, 21.

42. Information from a lecture given at the Smithsonian Institution by Elizabeth Loftus, Professor of Psychology/Adjunct Professor of Law, University of Washington, and from her book, *Eyewitness Testimony* (Cambridge: Harvard University Press, 1979).

43. Daniel Goleman, "In Memory, People Recreate Their Lives to Suit Their Images of the Present," *New York Times,* June 23, 1987, C-1.

44. Alan Baddeley, *Your Memory: A User's Guide* (New York: Macmillan, 1982), 68.

45. Boorstin, 384.

46. Baddeley, 44.

47. Baddeley, 55.

48. Hunter, 237–239.

49. Robert M. Butler, "Successful Aging and the Role of the Life Review," American Geriatrics Society, XXII:12 (December 1974), 530.

50. Walter Goodman, "How Alzheimer's Affects a Patient's Family, Too," *New York Times,* February 1, 1990, B-4

51. "The Facts of Life in Modern America," *Modern Maturity,* October–November 1987, 13.

52. Susan Okie, "Tangles in Brain Cells Believed to Hold Key," *Washington Post,* February 1, 1990, B-4.

53. Sandy Rovner, "With Age the Fear of Alzheimer's," *Washington Post* Health Section, December 30, 1986, 13.

54. Information from a lecture given at the Smithsonian Institution by Trey Sunderland, M.D., Chief, unit on Geriatric Psychopharmacology, National Institute of Mental Health.

55. Information from a lecture given by Herbert Weingartner, M.D., Chief, Cognitive Neuroscience Section, National Institute on Alcohol Abuse and Alcoholism.

56. Rosemary Dinnage, review of *When the Grass Was Taller* by Richard N. Coe, *Times Literary Supplement,* August 2, 1986, 14.

57. Patrick Huyghe, "Voices, Glances, Flashbacks: Our First Memories," *Psychology Today,* September 1985, 48.

58. Cohen lecture.

59. Sunderland lecture.

60. Jacobs, 15.

61. Harold M. Schmeck, Jr., "An Era Opens as Scientists Reproduce Drugs Found in the Body," *New York Times,* June 16, 1987, C-1.

62. Daniel Goleman, "Food and Brain: Psychiatrists Explore Use of Nutrients in Treating Disorders," *New York Times,* March 1, 1988, C-1.

63. Dan Halacy, *How to Improve Your Memory* (New York: Franklin Watts, 1977), 47.

64. Dan Halacy, 43.

65. Campbell, 207.

66. Source for many of the mnemonic devices: Michele Slung, *The Absent-Minded Professor's Memory Book* (New York: Ballantine Books, 1985).

Additional Reading

George Johnson. *In the Palaces of Memory: How We Build the Worlds Inside Our Heads.* New York: Knopf, 1991.

Elizabeth F. Loftus. *Witness for the Defense: The Accused, the Eyewitness and the Expert Who Puts Memory on Trial.* New York: St. Martin's Press, 1991.

A. R. Luria. *The Mind of a Mnemonist.* Cambridge: Harvard University Press, 1968.

Alan J. Parkin. *Memory and Amnesia.* Oxford & New York: Basil Blackwell, 1987.

Richard Restak. *The Brain Has a Mind of Its Own.* New York: Harmony Books, 1991.

Israel Rosenfield. *The Invention of Memory.* New York: Basic Books, 1989.

Oliver Sacks. *The Man Who Mistook His Wife for a Hat.* New York: HarperCollins, 1987.

Larry Squire and Nelson Butters, eds. *Neuropsychology of Memory.* New York: Guilford Press, 1984.

Frances A. Yates. *The Art of Memory.* Chicago: University of Chicago Press, 1974.

Index